PRESENTED TO:

_____

FROM:

_____

DATE:

_____

THE ENNEAGRAM COLLECTION

THE SUCCESSFUL ACHIEVER

ENNEAGRAM TYPE 3

BETH McCORD

Your **Enneagram** Coach

THOMAS NELSON

Since 1798

Enneagram Type 3: The Successful Achiever

© 2019 by Beth McCord

Published in Nashville, Tennessee, by Thomas Nelson. Thomas Nelson is a registered trademark of HarperCollins Christian Publishing, Inc.

Published in association with Alive Literary Agency.

Unless otherwise noted, Scripture quotations are taken from the ESV® Bible (The Holy Bible, English Standard Version®), copyright © 2001 by Crossway, a publishing ministry of Good News Publishers. Used by permission. All rights reserved.

Any Internet addresses, phone numbers, or company or product information printed in this book are offered as a resource and are not intended in any way to be or to imply an endorsement by Thomas Nelson, nor does Thomas Nelson vouch for the existence, content, or services of these sites, phone numbers, companies, or products beyond the life of this book.

Graphic Designer: Jane Butler, Well Refined Creative Director, wellrefined.co
Interior Designer: Emily Ghattas
Cover Designer: Greg Jackson at Thinkpen Design

ISBN-13: 978-1-4002-1572-0

Printed in China

19 20 21 22 23 GRI 10 9 8 7 6 5 4 3 2 1

Contents

Foreword   V

Introduction   XI

Overview of the Nine Enneagram Types   1

Overview of Type 3: The Successful Achiever   9

Day 1: Faith and the Enneagram   13

Day 2: Being Aware   21

Day 3: Core Motivations   27

Day 4: Core Fear   33

Day 5: Core Desire   39

Day 6: Core Weakness   45

Day 7: Core Longing   51

Day 8: Directional Signals of the Enneagram   57

Day 9: Levels of Alignment with God's Truth   61

CONTENTS

Day 10: When You Are Aligned   67

Day 11: When You Are Misaligned   71

Day 12: When You Are Out of

       Alignment Entirely   75

Day 13: The Wings   79

Day 14: The Triads   87

Day 15: Childhood Message   93

Day 16: Enneagram Paths   99

Day 17: Stress Path   105

Day 18: Blind Spot Path   111

Day 19: Growth Path   115

Day 20: Converging Path   121

Day 21: Moving Toward Your Best Self   127

Afterword   133

Acknowledgments   137

About the Author   141

Foreword

A few years ago, I recognized a pattern of *comparison* in my life. In particular, I noticed that comparisons were stealing my joy.

It would go something like this: I'd wake up in the morning and reach for my phone. What better way to begin your day than looking at your friends' food and baby pictures, right?

But after just a few minutes on Instagram, I didn't feel very good about myself. Have you ever landed on someone's feed and wished you were living their life in that moment? That was me.

I wound up comparing my latest vacation, new living room furniture, and career accomplishments to everyone else. And just like that, faster than you can type #blessed, I felt like I didn't measure up. I truly found that I was loving someone else's life and not my own.

Fast-forward to 2016 when the Enneagram came into my life. I had taken many different personality tests before, but the Enneagram quickly rose to the top as my favorite tool when it came to understanding myself and the people around me. A lot of other tests explain *how* you operate, but the Enneagram is the only test I've taken that explains *why* I operate the way I do. It opened my eyes to why comparison had become such a pattern in my life.

As it turns out, I'm Type 3: the Successful Achiever. When things are going well, I'm connecting with other people and really making progress toward my goals. But when my 3 is left unchecked, I can make myself miserable. I discovered that 3s tend to *compare ourselves to* and *compete with* others. We continually strive to be the very best. Go figure!

The Enneagram has revealed so much about my

personality that I wouldn't have picked up on without it.

And, to be honest, it's affected more than just me! It's also had a big impact on my relationships. For example, when my husband, Winston, read up on the Enneagram, he agreed that it was dead on for him too. (He's Type 5, by the way.) The whole Enneagram process has given us significant insights into not just ourselves but each other! Not to mention, both sides of our families now talk the Enneagram language, and I could not be happier about it.

After all, when you understand another person, you can empathize with them even if you don't see eye to eye. So it's really helped Winston and I navigate disagreements and made for a deeper connection in our marriage.

Now that I know about my Enneagram Type, a lot of other nuances in my life make sense. Like the first time Winston and I sat down to do a budget together as a married couple, I was the one dragging my feet. If you know what I do, that sounds crazy. I write and speak about money for a living, but budgeting never came naturally for me.

Once we got in the groove of creating a budget every month, though, I couldn't stop. I never loved *budgeting*, but I do love the *goals* it helps me achieve. As an Enneagram 3, a budget becomes a tool I can use to succeed.

Only when you understand yourself—your strengths, your weaknesses, and your motivations—can you grow. Our personalities shape our biases, expectations, and even our habits. So if we want to change those things, we need to become self-aware. The Enneagram has made that possible for me, along with significantly strengthening my relationships with others and my attitude toward myself.

But the best part for me is how it's made me more aware that God loves me for who I am, not for what I do. I can rest in the fact that I am loved by Jesus because I am His child—and that's it.

That's why I can't say enough about Beth McCord's take on the Enneagram. Her teachings paint a beautiful, detailed picture of who we are in Christ. This book reminds me of the unique message He has for me. It's by His accomplishments that my needs and desires are met—not my own.

Whether you're brand-new to the Enneagram or, like me, you already love it, this book will give you a deeper understanding of how God created you uniquely.

And how you can use the Enneagram to stop striving for success by everyone else's standards and start living a life *you* love.

Rachel Cruze, Bestselling Author, Radio & TV Personality, and Speaker

Introduction

I'm so glad you're here! As an Enneagram teacher and coach, I have seen so many lives changed by the Enneagram. This is a perfect place for you to start your own journey of growth. I'll explain how this interactive book works, but first I'd like to share a little of my story.

Before I learned about the Enneagram, I often unknowingly committed *assumicide*, which is my word for damaging a relationship by assuming I know someone's thoughts, feelings, and motivations. I incorrectly surmise why someone is behaving a particular way and respond (sometimes with disastrous results) without asking clarifying questions to confirm my assumptions or to find out what actually is going on. I've made many wrong and hurtful assumptions about people I dearly love, as well as destructive presumptions about myself.

When my husband, Jeff, and I were in the early years of our marriage, it was a difficult season in our relationship. For the life of me, I couldn't figure out Jeff, or myself. I had been a Christian since I was young and desired to live like Christ, but I kept running into the same stumbling blocks over and over again. I was constantly frustrated, and I longed to understand my heart's motives—*Why do I do what I do?* I figured understanding that might help jolt me out of my rut, but I didn't know where to start.

Then I learned about the insightful tool of the Enneagram, and it was exactly what I needed.

This personality typology (*ennea* for nine; *gram* for diagram) goes beyond what we do (our behaviors) and gets at *why* we do what we do (our heart's motives). And though there are just nine basic personality Types, each Type has multiple layers, allowing for numerous variations of any given personality Type.

The purpose of the Enneagram is to awaken self-awareness and provide hope for growth. Once we learn why each Type thinks, feels, and acts in specific ways, we can look at ourselves with new understanding. Then we can depend on God in new ways to reshape us. The Enneagram makes us aware of when our heart's motives are good and we are on the best path for our personality Type, and when our heart is struggling and veering off course. The Enneagram is an insightful tool, but God's truth is what sets us free and brings transformation.

When I first learned about the Enneagram, I resonated with the Type 9—and had a good laugh when I discovered that 9s know themselves the least! But I finally had wisdom that cleared away the fog and illuminated my inner world. I kept thinking, *Oh, that's why I do that!* Everything started making sense, which brought my restless heart relief.

The Enneagram also helped me see when my heart was aligned with God's truth, misaligned to some degree, or out of alignment entirely with the person God created me to be. It would highlight where I was misunderstanding myself or those I love, and then I could use that awareness to seek transformation. Using the Enneagram from this perspective was a significant turning point for me in all my relationships, especially my marriage. My new perspective allowed me to have more compassion, kindness, forgiveness, mercy, and grace toward others and myself.

Exploring my heart has been some of the hardest—and most rewarding—work I've ever done. The process of looking at our hearts exposes who we are at the core, which highlights our need for redemption and care from God, who is always supplying us with what we need. We simply need to come to Him and depend on Him to change us from the inside out. He will give us a new internal peace, joy, and security that will help us to flourish in new and life-giving ways. The Enneagram can function as an internal GPS, helping you understand why you and others think, feel, and behave in particular ways.

This internal GPS assists you in knowing your current location (your Main Enneagram Type) and your Type's healthiest destination (how your Type can live in alignment with the gospel).

The Enneagram also acts like a rumble strip on the highway—that boundary that makes an irritating sound when your car touches it, warning you when you're about to go off course. It keeps you from swerving into dangerous situations.

While everyone has character traits of all nine Types to varying degrees, we call only one our Main Type. In this book you will unlock some of the mysteries behind *why* you do what you do and discern ways you can grow into your best self.

If you're not sure of your Type number, that's okay! Going through the exercises will help you figure out what your Type number is. Sometimes it's helpful to find out what we're *not* as much as what we are. It's all about self-discovery and self-awareness.

If you find you resonate more with another number, that insight is valuable.

* * *

In the twenty-one entries that follow, we'll begin with a summary of your Type. Then we'll discuss topics that are general to the Enneagram and specific to your Type. Each reading will end with reflection questions—prompts to help you write out your thoughts, feelings, and gut reactions to what you have read. Putting pen to paper will help you focus and process what is going on inside you.

Before you begin, I want you to commit to observing your inner world from a nonjudgmental stance. Since God has fully forgiven us, we can observe ourselves without condemnation, guilt, or shame. Instead, we can rest in the fact that we are unconditionally loved, forgiven, and accepted based on what Christ did for us. Follow the prompts and write about your own story. Allow God to transform you from the inside out by helping you see yourself through the lens of the beautiful and amazing Type He designed you to be.

It's my privilege to walk with you as you discover who you are by examining your heart. I'm excited to be on this journey with you!

DEAR
TYPE 3
I'M THANKFUL FOR YOU BECAUSE...

You motivate others to be their best and can adapt to any given situation. You can recover quickly from setbacks, have the desire and will to improve yourself, and can easily forge a new path. Plus you are competent, work efficiently, and accomplish a lot quickly.

OVERVIEW OF THE NINE ENNEAGRAM TYPES

The Enneagram (*ennea* = nine, *gram* = diagram) is a map for personal growth that identifies the nine basic ways of relating to and perceiving the world. It accurately describes *why* you think, feel, and behave in particular ways based upon your Core Motivations. Understanding the Enneagram will give you more self-awareness, forgiveness, and compassion for yourself and others.

To find your main Type, take our FREE assessment at test.YourEnneagramCoach.com, and find the Type on the next page that has your Core Motivations—what activates and drives your thoughts, feelings, and behaviors.

Core Motivations of Each Type

 Core Desires: what you're always striving for, believing it will completely fulfill you

 Core Fears: what you're always avoiding and trying to prevent from happening

 Core Weakness: the issue you're always wrestling with, which will remain a struggle until you're in heaven and is a reminder you need God's help on a daily basis

 Core Longing: the message your heart is always longing to hear

Type 1: MORAL PERFECTIONIST

 Core Desire: Having integrity; being good, balanced, accurate, virtuous, and right.

 Core Fear: Being wrong, bad, evil, inappropriate, unredeemable, or corruptible.

 Core Weakness: *Resentment*: Repressing anger that leads to continual frustration and dissatisfaction with yourself, others, and the world for not being perfect.

 Core Longing: You are good.

Type 2: SUPPORTIVE ADVISOR

☀ **Core Desire:** Being appreciated, loved, and wanted.

▼ **Core Fear:** Being rejected and unwanted; being thought worthless, needy, inconsequential, dispensable, or unworthy of love.

⟳ **Core Weakness:** *Pride*: Denying your own needs and emotions while using your strong intuition to discover and focus on the emotions and needs of others; confidently inserting your helpful support in hopes that others will say how grateful they are for your thoughtful care.

🔥 **Core Longing:** You are wanted and loved.

Type 3: SUCCESSFUL ACHIEVER

☀ **Core Desire:** Having high status and respect; being admired, successful, and valuable.

▼ **Core Fear:** Being exposed as or thought incompetent, inefficient, or worthless; failing to be or appear successful.

⟳ **Core Weakness:** *Deceit*: Deceiving yourself into believing that you are only the image you present to others; embellishing the truth by putting on a polished persona for everyone (including yourself) to see and admire.

🔥 **Core Longing:** You are loved for simply being you.

Type 4: ROMANTIC INDIVIDUALIST

☀ **Core Desire:** Being unique, special, and authentic.

❗ **Core Fear:** Being inadequate, emotionally cut off, plain, mundane, defective, flawed, or insignificant.

⁑ **Core Weakness:** *Envy:* Feeling that you're tragically flawed, that something foundational is missing inside you, and that others possess qualities you lack.

🔥 **Core Longing:** You are seen and loved for exactly who you are—special and unique.

Type 5: INVESTIGATIVE THINKER

☀ **Core Desire:** Being capable and competent.

❗ **Core Fear:** Being annihilated, invaded, or not existing; being thought incapable or ignorant; having obligations placed upon you, or your energy being completely depleted.

⁑ **Core Weakness:** *Avarice:* Feeling that you lack inner resources and that too much interaction with others will lead to catastrophic depletion; withholding yourself from contact with the world; holding on to your resources and minimizing your needs.

🔥 **Core Longing:** Your needs are not a problem.

Type 6: LOYAL GUARDIAN

☀ **Core Desire:** Having security, guidance, and support.

▼ **Core Fear:** Fearing fear itself; being without support, security, or guidance; being blamed, targeted, alone, or physically abandoned.

♒ **Core Weakness:** *Anxiety*: Scanning the horizon of life and trying to predict and prevent negative outcomes (especially worst-case scenarios); remaining in a constant state of apprehension and worry.

♦ **Core Longing:** You are safe and secure.

Type 7: ENTERTAINING OPTIMIST

☀ **Core Desire:** Being happy, fully satisfied, and content.

▼ **Core Fear:** Being deprived, trapped in emotional pain, limited, or bored; missing out on something fun.

♒ **Core Weakness:** *Gluttony*: Feeling a great emptiness inside and having an insatiable desire to "fill yourself up" with experiences and stimulation in hopes of feeling completely satisfied and content.

 Core Longing: You will be taken care of.

Type 8: PROTECTIVE CHALLENGER

☀ **Core Desire:** Protecting yourself and those in your inner circle.

❗ **Core Fear:** Being weak, powerless, harmed, controlled, vulnerable, manipulated, and left at the mercy of injustice.

♻ **Core Weakness:** *Lust/Excess*: Constantly desiring intensity, control, and power; willfully pushing yourself on others in order to get what you desire.

🔥 **Core Longing:** You will not be betrayed.

Type 9: PEACEFUL MEDIATOR

☀ **Core Desire:** Having inner stability and peace of mind.

❗ **Core Fear:** Being in conflict, tension, or discord; feeling shut out and overlooked; losing connection and relationship with others.

♻ **Core Weakness:** *Sloth*: Remaining in an unrealistic and idealistic world in order to keep the peace, remain easygoing, and not be disturbed by your anger; falling asleep to your passions, abilities, desires, needs, and worth by merging with others to keep peace and harmony.

🔥 **Core Longing:** Your presence matters.

TYPE 3
KEY MOTIVATIONS

Threes are motivated by being admired and impressing others. They strive to hear affirmation and praise of what they have accomplished. In order for others to see them as valuable and respectable, they distinguish themselves through their accomplishments and achievements.

Overview of Type 3

The Successful Achiever

**Efficient | Accomplished | Motivating
Driven | Image-Conscious**

You are an optimistic, accomplished, and adaptable person who can achieve, excel, and reach ambitious goals with apparent ease and confidence.

However, in our fast-paced and comparison-driven society with limitless opportunities to excel, you struggle to keep up with the belief that you must be successful in every area of life. Burdened with the desire to appear accomplished and impress others, you live under constant pressure to measure your worth by external achievements and confidence.

Your deep fear of failing and being worthless or incapable causes you to struggle with deceit, hiding parts of yourself you don't want others to see and displaying only a successful exterior. In doing so, you become unaware of who you are authentically in your own heart, which impacts your relationships—with others and with yourself.

When you forget God's love for you, you can become excessively driven and image-conscious as you long for accomplishment and admiration. By constantly comparing yourself to others and being competitive and self-promoting, you run the risk of burnout and believing you are only as good as your last achievement.

However, when your heart aligns with God's truth, you believe you are loved and valued for who you really are, not just for your success and productivity. Your confidence, enthusiasm, and determination rub off on others and inspire them. You become a humble team player and a champion of others. Using your adaptability and drive for productivity and excellence, you accomplish incredible feats for the greater good.

Faith and the Enneagram

Is your heart a mystery to you? Do you need help using the knowledge the Enneagram offers to improve your life? If that's where you are, I'm happy to tell you that there is help and there is hope.

The Bible teaches that God cares about our heart's motives. He "sees not as man sees: man looks on the outward appearance, but the Lord looks on the heart" (1 Samuel 16:7). So we shouldn't look only at our external behaviors; we also need to examine our inner world. For most of us, it's no surprise that the heart of our problem is the problem of our heart!

Before we begin discussing the Enneagram in depth, I'd like to share my beliefs with you for two reasons: First, it's a critical part of how I'll guide you through the Enneagram principles. Second, my faith is what sustains and encourages me, and I believe the same will be true for you.

I believe the Bible is God's truth and the ultimate authority for our lives. Through it, we learn about God's character, love, and wisdom. It brings us close to Him and guides us in the best way to live. My relationship with God brought me healing and purpose before I ever heard of the Enneagram.

Jesus has not been optional for my personal growth; He has been absolutely and utterly vital. He has always come alongside me with love, compassion, and mercy.

I've always wanted my faith to be the most important part of my life, but I spent years frustrated, running into the same issues in my heart over and over again. The Enneagram helped me understand my heart's motives.

As you think about your Type, I'll help you look

at your heart, your life, and your relationships through the lens of the Enneagram. I'll also teach you ways to understand yourself and others and to develop patience and empathy for your differences.

With God working in you and helpful insights from the Enneagram to change awareness and actions, you'll grow into the person you'd like to be more than you've ever dared to dream possible.

When you place your faith in Jesus Christ as your Savior, three life-changing questions are answered, bringing you ultimate grace and freedom:

Am I fully accepted by God (even with all the mess and sin in my life)?

Yes! You are declared righteous. Christ not only purchased forgiveness for your sin but also gave you His perfect righteousness.

Am I loved by God?

Yes! God cherishes you and wants you to be close to Him. He adopted you, making you His beloved child.

Is it really possible for me to change?

Yes! You are being made new. This both *happened* to you and *is happening* to you. This means that you are changed because of what Christ has done, and you are continuing to change as you grow in Christ (it's a bit of a paradox). You can live in an ongoing process of growth by working with the Holy Spirit to become more like Christ, who loves you and gave Himself up for you.

These three life-changing events are what we mean by God's truth, the good news of Christ's finished work on our behalf—"the gospel."

Receiving God's truth and learning about the Enneagram will give you a deeper and richer understanding of *who you are* and *Whose you are*.

When we know *who we are*, we understand our heart's motives and needs and can see God reaching out to meet our needs and giving us grace for our sins through Christ.

And when we know *Whose we are*, we understand that, because of Christ's sacrifice on our behalf, we're God's cherished children. He comforts, sustains, and delights in us. Because of God's character, His love never changes; it doesn't depend on us "getting better" or "doing better" since it hinges solely on what Christ has already done for us. He loves us and desires for us to be in a relationship with Him. We become more like Him by surrendering to Him and depending on the Holy Spirit to transform us.

Which leads us back to looking at who we are. Bringing our faith and the Enneagram together helps us hear God's truths in our mother tongue (kind of like our personality Type's unique language), which enables us to understand God's truth more deeply and will lead to transformation.

Going Deeper

*What things have you longed to change about
yourself?*

_____

_____

_____

_____

_____

_____

_____

_____

_____

*How have you attempted to rescue yourself in the
past or bring about change on your own? How
successful were you?*

_____

_____

_____

What difference does knowing you belong to God make in your life?

Being Aware

We can't do anything to make God love us more or love us less since our relationship status has been taken care of solely through Christ's finished work on our behalf. And yet that doesn't mean we're not responsible for participating in our growth. That growth path will look different for different personality Types. We can use the Enneagram to help us find our unique path for transformation as we continue learning and growing. And that's what's super fun about the Enneagram! This insightful tool helps us discover *who we are* and *Whose we are.*

We are not alone on this journey of growth.

God is with us, sustaining us and providing for us. Although we're all uniquely made and no one is alike (it boggles the mind to think about it!), there are commonalities in how we think, feel, and act. The Enneagram shows us nine basic personality Types, each with its own specific patterns of thinking and ways of being: nine *valid* perspectives of the world. Getting to know each of these personality Types increases understanding, compassion, mercy, grace, and forgiveness toward ourselves and others.

Our creative God made us so diverse, yet we all reflect the essence of His character: wise, caring, radiant, creative, protective, insightful, joyful, knowledgeable, and peaceful. As we learn about ourselves and others from the Enneagram, we also learn more about God. Our strengths reflect His attributes.

So how do we begin to find our unique path for growth? By learning about the Enneagram, and by becoming aware of how our heart is doing, which isn't always easy for us. It takes a great deal of time and intentional focus. We start by observing our inner world from a *nonjudgmental* stance. (I don't know how to emphasize this enough!)

Then we can begin to recognize patterns, pause while we are in the present circumstance, and ask ourselves good, clarifying questions about *why* we are thinking, feeling, or behaving in particular ways. We can begin to identify those frustrating patterns we repeat over and over again (the ones we haven't been able to figure out how to stop) and start to think about why we keep doing them.

As I've said before, the Enneagram can act like a rumble strip on a highway, warning you when you're heading off your best path. It lets you know that if you continue in the same direction, drowsy or distracted, you might hurt yourself and others. Alerts about impending danger allow you to course correct, avoid heartache, and experience greater freedom. You will create new patterns of behavior, including a new way of turning to God, when you start to notice the rumble strips in your life.

When you're sensing a rumble strip warning, focus on the acronym AWARE:

- *Awaken*: Notice how you are reacting in your behavior, feelings, thoughts, and body sensations.
- *Welcome*: Be open to what you might learn and observe without condemnation and shame.
- *Ask*: Ask God to help clarify what is happening internally.
- *Receive*: Receive any insight and affirm your true identity as God's beloved child.
- *Enjoy*: Enjoy your new freedom from old self-defeating patterns of living.

Going Deeper

As you look back on your life, when would you have liked a rumble strip to warn you of danger?

_____

_____

_____

_____

_____

_____

In general, what causes you to veer off course and land in a common pitfall (for example, when you're worried)?

_____

_____

_____

_____

_____

SHARING WITH OTHERS HOW BEST TO LOVE ME

Affirm me by telling me that you like me and like being around me.

Express how proud you are of me and my achievements.

Please don't distract or interrupt me while I am working.

I welcome feedback as long as it is not overly critical or judgmental.

I thrive when my surroundings are harmonious, tidy, and peaceful.

Core Motivations

We'll begin discussing the fundamentals of the Enneagram by looking at our motivations.

Your Core Motivations are the driving force behind your thoughts, feelings, and actions. The internal motivations specific to your Type help explain why you do what you do. (This is why it's impossible to discern someone else's Type. We don't know what motivates them to think, feel, and behave in particular ways. It's their Core Motivations, not their actions, that determine their Type.)

These Core Motivations consist of:

- *Core Fear*: what you're always avoiding and trying to prevent from happening
- *Core Desire*: what you're always striving for, believing it will completely fulfill you
- *Core Weakness*: the issue you're always wrestling with, which will remain a struggle until you're in heaven and is a reminder you need God's help on a daily basis
- *Core Longing*: the message your heart longs to hear

The Enneagram, like a nonjudgmental friend, names and addresses these dynamics of your heart. When you use the Enneagram from a faith-centered approach, you can see how Christ's finished work on your behalf has already satisfied your Core Longing and resolved your Core Fear, Core Desire, and Core Weakness. It's a process to learn how to live in that reality.

When we stray from the truth that we are God's beloved children, it's harder to look inside. After all,

Scripture tells us that "the heart is deceitful . . . and desperately sick" (Jeremiah 17:9). When we forget God's unconditional love for us, we respond to our weaknesses and vulnerabilities with shame or contempt, leaving us feeling worse.

When we only focus on obeying externally, we attempt to look good on the outside but never deal with the source of all our struggles on the inside.

However, when we allow ourselves to rest in the truth that Christ took care of everything for us, we can look at our inner world without fear or condemnation. Real transformation begins when we own our shortcomings.

Here are the Core Motivations of a Type 3:

- *Core Fear*: being exposed as or thought incompetent, inefficient, or worthless; failing to be or appear successful
- *Core Desire*: having high status and respect; being admired, successful, and valuable
- *Core Weakness*: deceit; deceiving

yourself into believing you are only the image you present to others; embellishing the truth by putting on a polished persona for everyone (including yourself) to see and admire
- *Core Longing*: "You are loved for simply being you."

The Enneagram exposes the condition of our hearts, and it will tear down any facade we try to hide behind. Since we are God's saved children, we don't have to be afraid of judgment. We can be vulnerable because we know God has taken care of us perfectly through Christ—He has forgiven us and set us free from fear, condemnation, and shame. His presence is a safe place where we can be completely honest about where we are. With this freedom, allow the Enneagram to be a flashlight to your heart's condition. Let it reveal how you are doing at any given moment so you can remain on the best path for your personality Type.

Going Deeper

How challenging is it for you to look at the condition of your heart?

_____

_____

_____

_____

_____

_____

What response do you typically have when you recognize your struggles?

_____

_____

_____

_____

_____

_____

_____

How would you like to respond when the struggles inside you are exposed?

_____

_____

_____

_____

_____

_____

_____

_____

_____

_____

_____

_____

_____

_____

_____

_____

_____

_____

_____

_____

Core Fear

Understanding your Core Fear is the first step in identifying your motivations. Your personality believes it's vital to your well-being that you constantly spend time and energy avoiding this thing you fear. It is the lens through which you see the world, the "reality" you believe. You assume others do, or should, see the world through this lens, and you may become confused and dismayed when they don't.

Your Core Fear as a Type 3 is being exposed as or thought incompetent, inefficient, or worthless; failing to be or appear successful.

You don't want to fail or look lazy, be unprepared, or seem average to others. You don't want to be overshadowed, ask others for help, or be caught in embellishing the truth by putting on a polished persona for others to see.

Even though you fear being viewed as unsuccessful, here's what is true: all of Christ's accomplishments are now yours.

You do not need to chase after success or a particular image to have worth in this world because God accepts you as you are right now. When He looks at you, He sees His most precious child, credited with the achievements of Christ. Knowing your value to Him enables your heart to rest and exhale since there is no longer a need to fear failure. He gives you all you need and treasures you.

When your Core Fears get activated, use them as a rumble strip to alert you. Then pause, become AWARE, and reorient yourself with what is true so your heart can rest in His accomplishments.

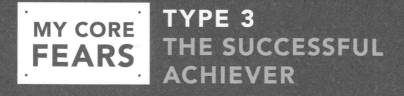

MY CORE FEARS

TYPE 3
THE SUCCESSFUL ACHIEVER

Being exposed as or thought incompetent, inefficient, or worthless; failing to be or appear successful

Going Deeper

*What comes to mind when you think about your
Core Fear?*

_____

_____

_____

_____

_____

_____

_____

*Do any particular words in the Type 3 Core Fear
description ring true for you?*

_____

_____

_____

_____

_____

_____

_____

What strategies have you used in the past to protect yourself from your fears?

_____

_____

_____

_____

_____

_____

_____

_____

_____

_____

_____

_____

_____

_____

_____

_____

_____

_____

_____

Core Desire

Understanding your Core Desire is the next step in identifying your motivations. Your Core Desire is what you're always striving for, believing it will ultimately fulfill you.

While your personality Type is running away from your Core Fear, it's also running toward your Core Desire. You believe that once you have this Core Desire met, all of life will be okay and you will feel fully satisfied and content. This longing to experience your Core Desire constantly propels you to focus your efforts on pursuing and obtaining it.

As a Type 3, you desire to have a high status and to be successful, admired, and valuable. You want to feel competent and accomplished, so you achieve lofty goals to gain attention, affirmation, and respect from others.

God knows your Core Desire, and He freely gives it to you. He gave you Jesus' high status and perfect accomplishments—not because you achieved anything, but because He values you and loves you. You can rest in having the greatest status there is and in God's complete affirmation of you.

Not everyone has the same Core Desire as you. Take time to recognize that others are just as passionate in obtaining their Core Desire as you are in gaining yours. This awareness will help you navigate relationship dynamics, enabling you to offer more empathy, compassion, and grace. Use the Enneagram to know yourself better so you can better communicate with others about what is happening inside your heart. Then be curious about others, and ask them to reveal to you their desires so you can get to know them on a deeper level.

MY CORE DESIRES

TYPE 3
THE SUCCESSFUL ACHIEVER

Having high status and respect; being admired, successful, and valuable

Going Deeper

As you look back over your life, what aspects of the Type 3 Core Desire have you been chasing?

_____

_____

_____

_____

_____

_____

_____

_____

Describe ways you have attempted to pursue these specific desires.

_____

_____

_____

_____

_____

_____

_____

_____

_____

_____

What would it feel like to trust in the fact that God has already met your Core Desire?

_____

_____

_____

_____

_____

_____

_____

_____

_____

_____

_____

_____

Core Weakness

Deep inside, you struggle with a Core Weakness, which is your Achilles' heel. This one issue repeatedly causes you to stumble in life. At times you might find some relief. But as hard as you try to improve on your own, your struggle in this area continually resurfaces.

God's encouraging words to you are that when you are weak, He is strong. This brings hope that you are not destined to be utterly stuck in your weakness. As you grow closer to God and depend on Him, He will lessen the constraint your Core Weakness has over you and help you move out of your rut.

As a Type 3, your Core Weakness is *deceit*. You deceive yourself into believing that you are only the image you present to others, and you embellish the truth by putting on a polished persona for everyone (including yourself). Feeling that you can only be loved by being or appearing accomplished, you avoid failure at all costs. You will shape-shift into any image that helps you appear successful and hide anything that doesn't conform to this image.

When you are struggling in life, you might double down on your efforts to appear successful through bragging, flaunting your accomplishments, dressing well, or owning expensive items. The more you struggle, the more your compulsion to create an idealized image intensifies.

The reality is, however, that God freely gives you Jesus' perfect status, because He values you for simply being His beloved child.

You must be exhausted from constantly striving for the next level of success and status. You can finally exhale and be your true self, without putting on "achieving masks" to earn love. God sees all of you, even the parts you want to hide, and still loves you deeply. You are free to be genuine and authentic.

Grounded in the truth that God gives you a high status, you no longer need to earn love and respect through your achievements and can focus on blessings others.

When you see your Core Weakness surfacing, think of it as a rumble strip, alerting you that you can easily veer off course into your common pitfalls of embellishing your accomplishments and shape-shifting into a charming and admirable persona in order to win others' approval and respect. Use this awareness to "recalculate" your inner world so you can get back to your healthiest path.

Going Deeper

What comes to mind as you think about your Core Weakness?

_____

_____

_____

_____

In what ways have you wrestled with deceit (embellishing your persona due to believing you are only the image you present to others)?

_____

_____

_____

_____

_____

_____

What specific things are you facing now that your Core Weakness impacts?

_____

_____

_____

_____

_____

_____

_____

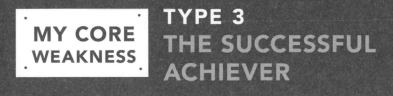

MY CORE WEAKNESS

TYPE 3
THE SUCCESSFUL ACHIEVER

Deceit — deceiving yourself into believing that you are only the image you present to others; embellishing the truth by putting on a polished persona for everyone (including yourself) to see and admire

Core Longing

Your Core Longing is the message your heart is always yearning to receive, what you've craved since you were a child. Throughout life, you've been striving to hear this message from your family members, friends, teachers, coaches, and bosses. No matter how much you've tried to get others to communicate this message to you, you've never felt it was delivered to the degree your heart needed it.

As a Type 3, your Core Longing is to hear, "You are loved for simply being you."

You have believed that if you could be successful and admirable enough, then others would communicate this message to you, whether in verbal or nonverbal ways. However, even those who have tried their best to do this for you are unable to satisfy this longing that runs so deep inside you.

Why? Because people *cannot* give you all you need. Only God can. When you're trying to receive this message apart from God, you will always thirst for more. But when you listen to Him and see that He's drawing you to Himself, then you will find fulfillment and freedom.

How does God meet your Core Longing?

1. He says you are valued.

God treasures you and made it possible for you to take on Jesus' perfect accomplishments as your own. You are valuable and cherished in the eyes of your Father.

2. He says you are loved for simply being you.

God created you to be your authentic self, not a fake or embellished image or persona. He calls you to rest in who you truly are and trust in His love for you without fearing what others think. Focus only on what He thinks of you. He loves you for simply being you!

When you feel worthless and exposed, use the Enneagram as the rumble strip to alert you of what is true: that you are valued and loved by God. Allow it to point out how you are believing false messages so you can live a more restful and authentic life.

Going Deeper

How have you seen your Core Longing at work in your life?

_____

_____

_____

_____

_____

_____

_____

What did that look like when you were a child?

_____

_____

_____

_____

_____

_____

_____

_____

_____

_____

_____

_____

_____

How does it appear in your life as an adult?

_____

_____

_____

_____

_____

_____

_____

_____

_____

_____

_____

_____

Describe how you feel and what you think when you read that God answers your longing.

_____

_____

_____

_____

_____

_____

_____

_____

_____

_____

_____

MY CORE LONGING

TYPE
THE SUCCESSFUL ACHIEVER

The message my heart always longs to hear.

"You are loved and valued
for simply being you."

Directional Signals of the Enneagram

Just as a GPS gives directional signals such as "Approaching right turn" or "Proceed to the high-lighted route," the Enneagram guides us in which way to go. But we still need to pay attention to where we're heading and reroute our course when necessary.

The Enneagram provides directions in a couple of ways: (1) by pointing out how aligned with God's truth we are, and (2) by showing us what other Types we are connected to and how we might take on those Types' characteristics in different life situations. We do not *become* the Types we are

YOUR INTERNAL GPS

It reveals **why** you think, feel, and behave in particular ways, so you can steer your internal life in the best direction for your personality Type.

connected to; we remain our Main Type (with its Core Fear, Desire, Weakness, and Longing) as we access the other Types' attributes.

The directional signals of the Enneagram make us aware of which way our heart is heading and where we might end up. Whether it's a good or bad direction depends on various factors—it can change day by day as we take on positive or negative qualities of other Types.

When we are headed in the wrong direction, the steps to turning around and getting back on track are simply owning our mistakes, turning from them, asking for forgiveness from God and others, and asking God to restore us to the best path.

The directional signals we'll discuss in the following entries are: the Levels of Alignment with God's Truth, the Wings, the Triads, and the Enneagram Paths. Hang in there! I'll guide you through these signals, which will help you discover who you are and Whose you are, and show you the healthiest path for your personality Type.

Type 3   **HOW I TYPICALLY COMMUNICATE**

When I am doing well, I am clear, straightforward, confident, motivated, efficient, focused on solutions, and encouraging.

When I am not doing well, I can be self-promoting, impatient with emotional or lengthy conversations, angry or short when frustrated, and not willing to fully disclose what's really going on inside.

Levels of Alignment with God's Truth

The first set of directional signals we'll discuss are the Levels of Alignment with God's truth. The inspiration for these levels comes from the apostle Paul, who wrote in Galatians 2:14 that some of the early Christian leaders' conduct was not in step (aligned) with God's truth. To grow in our particular personality Type, we must be in step with God's truth and design for us.

We all move fluidly through the Levels of Alignment from day to day. The level at which we find ourselves at any given moment depends on our heart's condition and how we're navigating through life.

Healthy	Aligned with God's Truth (Living as His Beloved)
Average (Autopilot)	Misaligned with God's Truth (Living in Our Own Strength)
Unhealthy	Out of Alignment with God's Truth (Living as an Orphan)

When we are resting, believing, and trusting in who we are in Christ, we are living as His beloved (healthy and aligned with God's truth). We are no longer using our personality strategies to meet our needs and desires. Instead, we are coming to our God, who we know loves us and will provide for us.

When our heart and mind begin to wander from that truth, we start to believe that we must take some control and live in our own strength, even though He is good and sovereign (average/auto-pilot level).

Then there are times when we completely forget that we are His beloved children. In this state of mind, we think we're all alone, that we're orphans who have to handle all of life on our own (unhealthy level).

But no matter where we are on the Levels of Alignment, we are always His cherished children. Christ's life, death, and resurrection accomplished everything required for us to be His. Therefore, no matter what state our heart is in, we can *rejoice* in His work in our lives, *repent* if we need to, and fully *rest* in who we are in Him.

As you can imagine, a group of people with the same personality Type (same Core Fear, Desire, Weakness, and Longing) can look vastly different from each other due to varying alignments with God's truth.

In the readings that follow, we will consider how you as a Type 3 function at the three Levels of Alignment.

Going Deeper

At what Level of Alignment do you think your heart is at the moment?

_____

_____

_____

_____

_____

_____

_____

In what season of life have you thrived the most, not feeling limited by your fears and weaknesses?

_____

_____

_____

_____

_____

_____

_____

What do you think contributed to that growth?

_____

_____

_____

_____

_____

_____

_____

_____

_____

_____

_____

_____

_____

_____

_____

_____

_____

_____

_____

_____

When You Are Aligned

When the condition of your heart is healthy, you align with God's truth that you are fully taken care of by Christ.

As a Type 3 at this level, you believe and trust your worth comes from being God's beloved child, not in your ability to create a successful image. You trust that it is safe to take off your "achieving masks" and allow your authentic self to be seen. You do this knowing that your self-worth and identity are now found solely in God.

Realizing that your self-worth and identity are now found solely in Jesus Christ, you no longer need to focus on yourself or how you can win people over.

You're free to focus on blessing others and helping them become the best versions of themselves. Still incredibly talented and good at setting goals, solving problems, and being efficient, you now use your strengths to benefit others, not simply for your gain.

You balance your work and personal life in a healthy way, and you are able to name and feel your emotions in a way that makes you more whole.

Going Deeper

When are you at your best and most trusting of God?

_____

_____

_____

_____

_____

_____

_____

What differences do you notice in your thinking and in your life when you're in that state?

_____

_____

_____

_____

_____

_____

_____

_____

What helps you stay in alignment with God's plan for your personality Type?

_____

_____

_____

_____

_____

_____

_____

_____

Write about a time when you've exhibited true patience and empathy for others and benefiting others over your own self gain.

When You Are Misaligned

Even though we know God is good and in control, there are times when our hearts and minds wander away from the truth that God loves us and has fully provided for us in the finished work of Christ on our behalf. In this average or autopilot level of health, we start to believe that we must take some control and live in our own strength.

As a Type 3 at this level, you believe you must earn love. You go into overdrive, becoming extremely focused on being the best in every category of life to gain admiration and respect. You rely more on your "superpower" of shape-shifting into whatever a situation calls for. Displaying great confidence, you

MY **HIDDEN** STRUGGLE
TYPE 3

The need to appear polished,
productive, and look like I
have it all together

A constant internal pressure
to be successful and perform
at maximum efficiency

Deep anxiety about my
value and doubting that I
can be truly loved for
simply being myself

place a lot of attention on accomplishing goals and being productive and efficient.

In your pursuit of success, you put your emotions out of reach from yourself and others, which puts a strain on your relationships. Transparency and authenticity, which are critical for relationships to thrive, become difficult for you.

Desiring to impress others, you constantly promote yourself and make yourself sound better than you are. This can inadvertently push away others instead of drawing them closer.

Going Deeper

What aspects of your behavior and life indicate that you are becoming misaligned?

_____

_____

_____

_____

_____

In what ways do you attempt to live in your own strength, not in your identity as a person God loves?

_____

_____

_____

_____

_____

_____

_____

_____

What can you do when you begin to catch yourself in misalignment?

_____

_____

_____

_____

_____

_____

_____

When You Are Out of Alignment Entirely

When we completely forget that our status never changes and we are still His beloved based on what Christ did for us, we think and believe we're all alone, like an orphan.

Your whole world at this level revolves around your accomplishments and other people's opinions of you due to forgetting your true identity in Christ. To gain admiration and love from others, you fabricate stories about yourself and your achievements, never admit when you are wrong, and do anything to present a favorable persona.

Refusing to reveal anything that might diminish

your image means keeping others from knowing who you really are. This image management is exhausting, and you never feel you get enough applause.

If this continues, you can become extremely competitive, mean, and vengeful, only looking out for yourself. To avoid exposure of your wrongdoings, you become devious and deceptive. You shift the blame onto others, and people will believe you because you are so charming and convincing. You become untrustworthy, maliciously betraying or sabotaging people to triumph over them.

This cycle will continue until you realize that God is a loving and caring Father to you. When you begin to believe this truth and depend on Him completely, you will move up the levels of health.

Going Deeper

In what seasons of life have you been most out of alignment with God's truth?

_____

_____

_____

_____

_____

_____

_____

What does this level look like for you (specific behaviors, beliefs, etc.)?

_____

_____

_____

_____

_____

_____

_____

Who in your life can best support and encourage you when you're struggling and guide you back to health?

The Wings

The next set of directional signals we'll discuss are the Wings, which are the two numbers *directly* next to your Main Type's number on the Enneagram diagram. As I've said, we access the characteristics of the Type on either side of us while remaining our Main Type. So everyone's Enneagram personality is a combination of one Main Type and the two Types adjacent to it.

As a Type 3, your Wings are 2 and 4. You'll often see it written this way: 3w2 or 3w4.

Everyone uses their Wings to varying degrees and differently in different circumstances, but it's common for a person to rely more on one Wing than another.

You can think of the Wings like salt and pepper. Each Wing adds a unique "flavor" to your personality, bringing complexity to your Main Type. Just as a delicious filet mignon doesn't *become* the salt or pepper we season it with, we don't become our Wings. Our Wings influence our Main Type in varying ways, both positively and negatively depending on where we are on the Levels of Alignment. We know that too much salt or pepper can make that filet inedible, but the right balance can enhance our enjoyment of it significantly.

When we align with God's truth, we can access the healthy aspects of our Wings. When we are misaligned or out of alignment with God's truth, we will often draw from the average or unhealthy aspects of our Wings. And like under seasoning or over seasoning our perfectly cooked steaks, it can make a huge difference.

Learning how to use our Wings correctly can dramatically alter our life experiences. Applying "seasoning"—utilizing the healthy attributes of our Wings—can help us change course. As we return to believing and trusting in God, we can express ourselves more fully and be seen for who we really are.

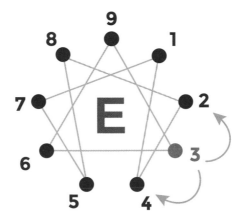

Type 3 with Wing 2 (3w2), The Star: These two Types complement one another with impressive interpersonal skills. They are incredibly charming, likable, adaptable, and engaging. They are confident and popular, strive to have physical attractiveness, and enjoy the spotlight.

If you're a Star, you are emotionally friendly, talkative, and demonstrative toward others. The Type 2 in you brings a warmer touch. More people-oriented and generous, you serve and accomplish for others since you need to be admired, and you can turn on the charm to get the affirmation you long for. You can struggle with comparison, competitiveness, and needing others (particularly family) to reflect well on you.

Type 3 with Wing 4 (3w4), The Professional: Types 3 and 4 are at odds with each other internally. Type 3 puts on a persona to charm others and win admiration, but Type 4 demands authenticity and realness. Type 3 is more interpersonal, while Type 4 is more withdrawn.

If you're a Professional, you are reserved, private, quiet, and focused on achieving recognition through your work and personal status. You can express yourself through creativity, aesthetics, and being more emotionally vulnerable.

Type 3s need to achieve and impress combined with Type 4s feeling of inadequacy causes the

Type 3 WINGS

Type 3 with 2 Wing (3w2)
"The Star"
They are warmer, more encouraging, sociable, popular, enjoy being center of attention, and seductive.

Type 3 with 4 Wing (3w4)
"The Professional"
They are more focused on work, success, and introspection. They are more sensitive, artistic, imaginative, and pretentious.

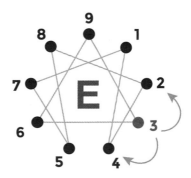

Professional to fear failure more than the Star does.
You need others to see your success and affirm you
in order to feel okay.

Going Deeper

Which Wing do you use more?

_____

_____

_____

_____

_____

_____

_____

*How have you seen this Wing enhance your
Main Type?*

_____

_____

_____

How does it impact your relationships, work, and everyday life?

How does the other Wing influence your Main Type?

_____

_____

_____

_____

_____

_____

_____

How can you utilize it more to create balance?

_____

_____

_____

_____

_____

_____

_____

_____

_____

The Triads

The next set of directional signals we'll discuss are the Triads. We can group the nine personality Types in many ways, and the most common one is by groupings of three, or Triads. The three Types in each group share common assets and liabilities. For each person one Triad is more dominant (the one with your Main Type) than the other two.

Though we could name several different Triads within the Enneagram, the best known is the Center of Intelligence Triad:

- Feeling Center (Heart Triad): Types 2, 3, and 4
- Thinking Center (Head Triad): Types 5, 6, and 7
- Instinctive Center (Gut Triad): Types 8, 9, and 1

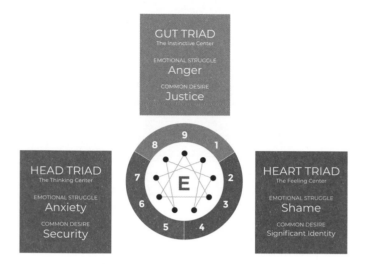

Two commonalities drive the Enneagram Types in each of these three centers: a common emotional imbalance and a common desire.

In the Heart Triad, Types 2, 3, and 4 are *imbalanced* in their *feelings*. This group shares similar assets and liabilities surrounding their feelings as well as engaging in life and circumstances through their feelings. Type 2s feel other people's emotions. Type 3s access their emotions the least, concerned that those emotions will hinder them from accomplishing goals and tasks. Type 4s feel all their emotions with depth and intensity. Those in the Heart Triad share a reaction to their *emotional struggle* with *shame*.

Those in the Heart Triad focus on a desire for a *specific identity or significance* that they want others to see and recognize. Type 2s want to be seen as the most supportive, caring, and selfless person. Type 3s want to be seen as the most successful, admirable, and accomplished person. And Type 4s want to be seen as special, different, and unique.

When you are healthy as a Type 3, you improve yourself, motivate others to be their best, and adapt to any given situation. You have a strong sense of self and can remain positive for a long time.

However, when you begin to struggle, you adjust your self-image to the particular needs of any group and become whatever successful persona is called for. You earn the reward of admiration for your performance, charm, and accomplishments. This requires you to put your feelings and true identity

ENNEAGRAM TYPE 3

At Their Best	At Their Worst
Optimistic	Deceptive
Self-Affirming	Self-Promoting
Industrious	Pretentious
Efficient	Vain
Self-Propelled	Superficial
Energetic	Exploitative
Goal-Orienting	Overly Competitive
Team Builder	Workaholic
Motivator	Attention Getting

aside, causing you to lose touch with your authentic self and your heart's desires. You feel it is necessary to gain others' respect to avoid feeling shame.

Going Deeper

What stands out to you about being in the Feeling Triad and your propensity for feelings of shame?

How attuned are you to your thinking and gut instincts in comparison to feelings?

In what ways do you wrestle with shame and constantly feel the need to shape-shift into an admirable image?

_____

_____

_____

_____

_____

Do your efforts to shape-shift bring the acceptance and love you want?

_____

_____

_____

_____

Where do your strengths of efficiency and high achievement shine the most?

_____

_____

_____

_____

Childhood Message

Before we discuss the last set of directional signals (the Enneagram Paths), we need to understand what the Enneagram calls a Childhood Message.

From birth, everyone has a unique perspective on life, our personality Type's perspective. We all tend toward particular assumptions or concerns, and these develop into a Childhood Message. Our parents, teachers, and authority figures may have directly communicated this message to us, but most of the time, we interpreted what they said or did through the lens of our personality Type to fit this belief.

Sometimes we can see a direct correlation between our Childhood Message and a childhood event; other times we can't. Somewhere, some-how, we picked up a message that rang true for us because of our personality Type's hardwiring. This false interpretation of our circumstances was and still is painful to us, profoundly impacting us as children and as adults.

Gaining insight into how our personality Type interpreted events and relationships in childhood will help us identify how that interpretation is impacting us today. Believing our Childhood Message causes our personality to reinforce its strategies to protect us from our Core Fear—apart from God's truth. Once we understand that the message is hardwired into our thinking, we can experience God's healing truth and live more freely.

What's more, when we know the Childhood Message of others, we can begin to understand why they do what they do and how we can communicate with them more effectively.

As a Type 3, your Childhood Message is: "It is not okay to have your own feelings or identity."

The message your heart longed to hear as

a child is your Core Longing: "You are loved for simply being you."

• • •

Type 3s grew up believing that it was not okay to have their own feelings or identity. They sensed or were told that they needed to set aside their real selves to become successful and admirable.

They inferred this message to mean, "You are what you do." So they became fixated on performing and excelling so that others would see their accomplishments and express amazement.

These children ultimately feared that their parents, friends, coaches, and other important figures would overlook or forget them if they did not excel in every area of life. This fear led them to become the best in anything they attempted in life.

Type 3 children woke up in the morning knowing what they needed to wear to make a good impression. They were socially adept and knew which kids they needed to be with to gain the status they craved.

They tended to show off and exaggerate their achievements to get applause and respect from others. If they didn't tell someone about what they accomplished, then they couldn't receive the praise they sought.

Type 3s are focused and competitive because they believe only winners are loved.

Knowing your personality Type's Childhood Message will help you break free from childhood perceptions and reinterpret pieces of your story from a better vantage point. As you explore this, be gracious to yourself and your past. Be sensitive, nonjudgmental, caring, and kind to yourself. And remember, only God can fully redeem your past. He can free you from chains that bind, heal wounds that linger, and restore you to freedom.

Going Deeper

To what degree do you relate to the Type 3 Childhood Message?

_____

_____

_____

_____

_____

_____

_____

What stories come to mind when you hear it?

_____

_____

_____

_____

_____

_____

_____

_____

What circumstances in the present have repeated this message from the past?

_____

_____

_____

_____

_____

_____

_____

What advice would you give to your childhood self in light of this message?

_____

_____

_____

_____

_____

_____

_____

_____

Enneagram Paths

The final directional signals we'll discuss are the Enneagram Paths, which the inner lines and arrows in the Enneagram diagram display. The lines and arrows going out from our Main Type point to our Connecting Types. As a Type 3, you connect to Types 9 and 6.

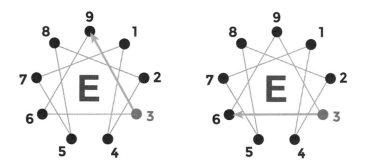

Remember, we can access both positive and negative characteristics of a Type we are connected to. The kind we access depends on whether we are aligned, misaligned, or out of alignment with God's truth.

Here is an overview of the four Enneagram Paths, which we'll discuss further in the following readings:

- *Stress Path*: When we're under stress, we tend to take on some of the misaligned or out-of-alignment characteristics of our Stress Path Type. For Type 3, these are the negative aspects of Type 9.
- *Blind Spot Path*: When we're around those we're most familiar with (mainly family), we display the misaligned characteristics of our Blind Spot Path Type. We typically do not see these characteristics in ourselves easily. For Type 3, these are the negative aspects of Type 6.
- *Growth Path*: When we believe and trust

that God loves us and that all He has is ours in Christ, we begin to move in a healthier direction, accessing the aligned characteristics of our Connecting Type. For Type 3, these are the positive aspects of Type 6.

- *Converging Path*: After making progress on the Growth path, we can reach the most aligned point of our Type, which is where three healthy Types come together. Here we access the healthiest qualities of our Main Type, our Growth Path's Type, and our Stress Path's Type.

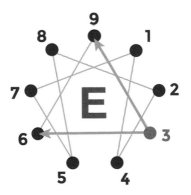

Going Deeper

In what direction is your heart currently heading?

_____

_____

_____

_____

_____

_____

_____

What concerns are you wrestling with?

_____

_____

_____

_____

_____

_____

_____

_____

What growth have you experienced recently?

When you look at the four paths, what path have you been traveling recently? Why?

Stress Path

Under stress, you tend to move in the direction of the arrow below, taking on some of the misaligned characteristics of Type 9. Learning to identify these behavior patterns can serve as a rumble strip warning that you're veering off course. Then you can

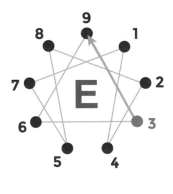

stop, pray for God's help, and move in a healthier direction for your personality.

As a Type 3 moving toward the average or unhealthy Type 9, you may:

- suddenly shut down, becoming disengaged, apathetic, and passive.
- remain busy to avoid looking lazy, even if you're not able to focus.
- withdraw and become depressed, losing interest in what you need to accomplish.
- want to be left alone and not bothered.
- numb out by watching TV, playing video games, shopping, eating, etc.
- stubbornly resist help from others or even hearing that you need help.

Going Deeper

Describe a stressful time when you took on some of these tendencies.

_____

_____

_____

_____

_____

_____

_____

What was the situation, and why were you triggered to respond this way?

_____

_____

_____

_____

_____

_____

When have you used numbing behaviors to cope with stress and feeling overwhelmed?

_____

_____

_____

_____

_____

_____

_____

_____

_____

_____

What tendencies do you notice about yourself in times of stress?

_____

_____

_____

_____

_____

What things in your life cause the most stress for you?

TYPE 3 UNDER STRESS

When under stress, **Type 3** will start to exhibit some of the average to unhealthy characteristics of **Type 9**.

Becoming disengaged, apathetic, and going on "autopilot"

Losing focus and drive, they involve themselves with busywork to give the appearance of accomplishment

Feeling little energy and passion, they want to be left alone and given their space

Blind Spot Path

When you're around people you're most familiar with—family members or close friends—you express yourself more freely. You show them parts of yourself you don't show anyone else, for better or worse. When you're uninhibited and not at your best, you display the negative qualities of your personality. On this Blind Spot Path, you access the misaligned attributes of your Connecting Type, which is Type 6.

You may be unaware that you're behaving differently with your family members or close friends than you are with other people. Be sure to take note of this path when you're trying to understand yourself and your reactions, because it may surprise you. Working on these negative aspects can improve the relationship dynamics with those you're closest to.

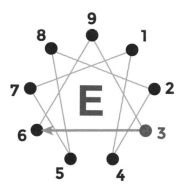

As a Type 3 moving toward the average or unhealthy Type 6, you may:

- express your anxieties and frustrations.
- complain and display negative attitudes you don't typically reveal to others.
- vent your dissatisfactions, self-doubt, dread, and anger.

- react strongly when blamed for or accused of something.
- become suspicious of others and unsure of whom you can trust.

Going Deeper

How do you respond when you feel overwhelmed in the presence of people you feel secure with versus those you're less comfortable with?

_____

_____

_____

_____

_____

_____

_____

_____

_____

_____

Which of the average or unhealthy tendencies do you resonate with the most?

_____

_____

_____

_____

_____

_____

_____

Describe a situation where you reacted in the ways described above.

_____

_____

_____

_____

_____

_____

_____

_____

Growth Path

When you believe and trust that God loves you, and all He has is yours, you begin to relax and let go of your personality's constraints and lies. You draw nearer to Him and move in a direction that aligns you with His truth. You feel safe, secure, and loved.

Feeling more joy, peace, and liberation, you stretch yourself toward healthier attributes, even though it is hard. As you grow in faith and depend solely on Him, God blesses you with real and lasting transformation, shaping you into who He made you to be.

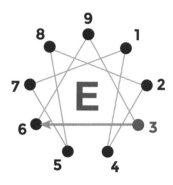

As a Type 3 moving toward the healthy side of Type 6, you can:

- rest knowing that Christ's accomplishments are now yours.
- become less competitive and more corporative.
- become more loyal, cooperative, and focused on the well-being of others.
- shift to a team-player mind-set, using your talents to help others and raise their status.
- ask for help and advice.
- be more vulnerable and reveal who you are behind any "achieving masks."
- be aware of your feelings and express them to others more freely.

Going Deeper

When you are growing, what changes about your heart and your typical responses?

_____

_____

_____

_____

_____

_____

Which of these growth attributes would you love to experience more in your life?

_____

_____

_____

_____

_____

_____

_____

What helps to support your growth and flourishing?

_____

_____

_____

_____

_____

_____

_____

_____

_____

How can you incorporate those things into your life more?

_____

_____

_____

_____

_____

_____

_____

_____

TYPE 3 DIRECTION OF GROWTH

When moving in the direction of growth, **Type 3** will start to exhibit some of the healthier characteristics of **Type 6**.

Becoming more cooperative and committed to others

Becoming more vulnerable

Becoming aware of their feelings and revealing who they are behind their "achieving" masks

Converging Path

You are your best self on the Converging Path, where three Types come together. Here you access the healthiest qualities of your Main Type, your Growth Path's Type, and your Stress Path's Type. When you live in the fullness of who you really are in Christ, you are freed from the bonds of your personality.

This path of personal transformation can be difficult to reach and maintain. When you first learn about the Converging Path, you may feel it's too hard to travel. But God wants to provide this path for you. Trust Him, follow Him, and ask Him to be with you as you move forward.

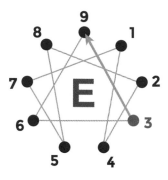

As a Type 3 moving toward the healthy side of Type 9, you may:

- learn how to *be*, instead of constantly doing, achieving, and performing.
- excel out of joy rather than desperate need or fear.
- value the viewpoints of others and appreciate their contributions.
- seek to collaborate rather than doing things yourself.
- search for ways to support others and their success instead of needing to stand out.
- relax and rest more, knowing your identity isn't tied to what you accomplish.

Going Deeper

Can you recall a time when you experienced the freedom and joy of the Converging Path?

_____

_____

_____

_____

_____

What was it like when you accessed the healthiest aspects of your Main Type, Growth Path's Type, and Stress Path's Type?

_____

_____

_____

_____

_____

_____

What would help you move toward your Converging Path more often?

_____

_____

_____

_____

_____

_____

_____

_____

_____

_____

_____

_____

_____

_____

_____

_____

_____

_____

_____

Spiritual Renewal

TYPE 3
THE SUCCESSFUL ACHIEVER

GOING DEEPER

Grab a journal, and instead of writing your goals or to-do lists, list all the ways you are valuable outside of the things you accomplish. Get in touch with your true feelings, and ask yourself if you're projecting a false image, avoiding negative emotions, or neglecting important relationships for the sake of being successful. Reflect on the truth that you are loved by God, not for anything you do, but for who you really are.

Moving Toward Your Best Self

The journey of exploring your heart is not an easy one, but it's an exciting one.

God has a unique message for each Type. The message He tells you as a Type 3 is: "You are loved for just being you. You do not need to perform to earn My love."

You already have the perfect status you are striving for because Christ accomplished it for you and gave it to you. You are free from the lie that you have to be the best in every area of life. He was the best on your behalf. You do not need to earn love; it was freely given to you.

You are not what you do. You are God's child,

and He deeply cherishes you for exactly who you are. He sees you completely (weaknesses, frailties, strengths, successes, failures) and pursues you with His great love. Open your heart, feel His warm embrace, and engage your emotions. This is where your authentic self will come forth.

Do not be afraid of raw emotions. They may feel uncomfortable and unproductive, but the opposite is true. In time, as you embrace them, they will allow you to love yourself, others, and God in deeper and richer ways.

Each Type has a signature Virtue, which you exhibit when you are at your best, and Type 3s Virtue is *truthfulness/authenticity.*

At your best, you do not need the constant applause and admiration of others because you know you are loved for simply being yourself. You will still bless others with your incredible talents of efficiency and productivity, but you will do it with honesty and authenticity, and for the sake of others, not simply for your gain.

You are fully living out your true identity in

Christ, able to reveal your authentic self without fear, knowing you are deeply loved for who you truly are in Christ. You become self-accepting and gentle. You can stretch yourself by being modest and charitable, and allowing your authentic emotions to emerge in front of others.

Using the Enneagram from a biblical perspective can empower you to see yourself with astonishing clarity so you can break free from self-condemnation, fear, and shame by experiencing unconditional love, forgiveness, and freedom. In Him, you are whole. And with Him by your side, you can grow stronger and healthier every day.

Now that you know how to use this internal GPS and its navigational signals, start using it every day. Tune in to how your heart is doing. Avoid your common pitfalls by staying alert to your rumble strips. As you learn new awareness and actions, you will move forward on the path that is healthiest for your personality Type and experience the gift of tremendous personal growth.

Going Deeper

What do you notice about yourself when you're at your best?

_____

_____

_____

_____

_____

_____

What would the world be like without the involvement of healthy Type 3s?

_____

_____

_____

_____

_____

_____

 **VIRTUE**

Truthfulness is your virtue.

Truly being yourself enables you to love others simply and genuinely. Being yourself shows real love.

What are some practical ways you can offer your virtue to others today?

Afterword

God's plan to restore the world involves all of us, which is why He made us so vastly different from each other in ways that reflect who He is.

That is why I'm so thrilled you picked up this book and have done the hard, but rewarding, work of looking into your heart. When you align with God's truth, you can support the kingdom, knit people together, and be the best *you* only you can be.

Growth is *not* easy. It requires us to surrender to God, depend on Him, and walk into His calling for us. But when we let go of our control and He takes over, He will satisfy our hearts, filling them with His goodness, and His blessings will flow into our lives and others' lives.

I can attest to God's transformative work having this ripple effect—reaching and positively impacting different parts of our lives and everyone we encounter. As I became more aligned with God's truth (and make no mistake, I'm still in progress!), the changes I was making helped transform my relationships with Jeff, my family, and other people around me. More and more friends, acquaintances, and even strangers were experiencing the transformation that comes from God through the tool of the Enneagram.

I can't wait to look back a year from now, five years from now, or even a decade from now, and hear about the ripple effects *your* transformation has created for hope, wholeness, and freedom. I'm excited about the path of discovery and growth ahead of you! What is God going to do in you with this new understanding of yourself and those around you? What are the things you'll hear Him whisper in your heart that will begin to set you free?

And how will your personal transformation bring positive change to the people in your life?

This is what I hope for you: First, that you will believe and trust in your identity in Christ. In Him, you are forgiven and set free. God delights in having you as His dear child and loves you unconditionally. This reality will radically change everything in you—it is the ultimate transformation from death to life.

Second, I hope that as you discover more about your Enneagram Type, you'll recognize how your personality apart from Christ is running *away* from your Core Fear, running *toward* your Core Desire, *stumbling* over your Core Weakness, and *desperate* to have your Core Longing met. As you become aware of these traits, you can make them the rumble strip alarms that point out what's going on in your heart. Then you can ask the Holy Spirit to help you navigate your inner world and refocus your efforts toward traveling the best path for your personality Type.

Third, I hope that God will reveal to you, both

in knowledge and experience, the transformative work of the Holy Spirit. With Him you can move toward growth, using all the tools of the Enneagram (the Levels of Alignment, the Wings, the Triads, the Enneagram Paths, etc.) to bring out the very best in you, the way God designed you to be. As a result, others will be blessed, God will be glorified, and you will experience the closeness of a Savior who will always meet your every longing and need.

May the love of Christ meet you where you are and pull you closer to God and others. And may you experience the joy of knowing His love for you in a deeper and more meaningful way.

Acknowledgments

My husband: I have to start by thanking my incredible husband, Jeff, who is my biggest cheerleader and supporter. He has helped me use the Enneagram from a biblical perspective and lovingly ensured that I expanded my gifts. Without his encouragement each step of the way, I never would have ventured into this world of writing. Thank you so much, Jeff.

My kids: Nathan and Libby McCord, you are a gift and blessing to me, and an inspiration for the work I do. Thank you for affirming me, being patient with me, and always believing in me. I pray this resource will bless you back as you journey through life.

My family: To my incredible parents, Dr. Bruce and Dana Pfuetze, who have always loved me well and encouraged me to move past difficulties by relying on the Lord. To my dear brother and sister-in-law, Dr. Mark and Mollie Pfuetze, thank you for being a source of support.

My team at Your Enneagram Coach: You enable me to be the best I can be as a leader, and I'm so honored to be a part of our amazing team. Thank you for letting me serve, for showing up every day, and for helping those who want to become more like Christ by using the Enneagram from a biblical perspective. Thank you, Danielle Smith, Traci Lucky, Robert Lewis, Lindsey Castleman, Justin Barbour, and Monica Snyder.

My marketing team, Well Refined Co.: Thank you, Christy Knutson, Jane Butler, JoAnna Brown, and Madison Church.

My agent: Thank you, Bryan Norman, for helping me navigate through all the ins and outs so that this could be the very best work for our readers. Your advice was most beneficial.

My publisher: To Adria Haley and the team at HarperCollins Christian, thank you for allowing me to share my passion for the Enneagram with the world in such a beautiful way through this book collection.

My writing team at StrategicBookCoach.com: Thank you, Danielle Smith, Karen Anderson, and Sharilyn Grayson for helping me create my manuscript.

My friend and advisor: Writing a book is harder than I expected and more rewarding than I could have ever imagined. None of this would have been possible without my most-cherished friend and beloved advisor, Karen Anderson. I am thankful for her heart, her passion, and her help every step of the way. You beautifully take my concepts and make them sing. Thank you!

About the Author

Beth McCord has been using the Enneagram in ministry since 2002 and is a Certified Enneagram Coach. She is the founder and Lead Content Creator of Your Enneagram Coach and cowrote *Becoming Us: Using the Enneagram to Create a Thriving Gospel-Centered Marriage* with her husband, Jeff. Beth has been featured as an Enneagram expert in magazines and podcasts and frequently speaks at live events. She and Jeff have two grown children, Nate and Libby, and live in Franklin, Tennessee, with their blue-eyed Australian Shepherd, Sky.

Continue Your Personal Growth Journey *Just for Type 3!*

Get your Type's in-depth online coaching course that is customized with guide sheets and other helpful insights so you can continue uncovering your personal roadmap to fast-track your growth, overcome obstacles, and live a more fulfilling life with God, others, and yourself.

VISIT YOURENNEAGRAMCOACH.COM/EXPLORING-YOU

The mission of YourEneagramCoach.com is for people to see themselves with astonishing clarity so they can break free from self-condemnation, fear, and shame by knowing and experiencing unconditional love, forgiveness, and freedom in Christ.